My Dad

D1785722

Story by Monica Hughes
Pictures by Colin Mier

OXFORD
UNIVERSITY PRESS

Dad put on **big** trousers.

2

3

Dad put on **big** boots.

5

Dad put on a **big** jacket.

Dad put on a **big** hat.

9

Dad put on **big** gloves.

11

Dad got on a **big** fire engine.